I0019631

N.B. Mahesh Kumar
Dr. K. Premalatha

Finger Knuckle-Print Authentication Using Fast Discrete Orthonormal Stockwell Transform

Anchor Academic
Publishing

Kumar, N.B. Mahesh, Premalatha, K.: Finger Knuckle-Print Authentication Using Fast Discrete Orthonormal Stockwell Transform, Hamburg, Anchor Academic Publishing 2017

Buch-ISBN: 978-3-96067-203-6
PDF-eBook-ISBN: 978-3-96067-703-1
Druck/Herstellung: Anchor Academic Publishing, Hamburg, 2017

Bibliografische Information der Deutschen Nationalbibliothek:
Die Deutsche Nationalbibliothek verzeichnet diese Publikation in der Deutschen Nationalbibliografie; detaillierte bibliografische Daten sind im Internet über http://dnb.d-nb.de abrufbar.

Bibliographical Information of the German National Library:
The German National Library lists this publication in the German National Bibliography. Detailed bibliographic data can be found at: http://dnb.d-nb.de

© Anchor Academic Publishing, Imprint der Diplomica Verlag GmbH
Hermannstal 119k, 22119 Hamburg
http://www.diplomica-verlag.de, Hamburg 2017
Printed in Germany

TABLE OF CONTENTS

CHAPTER 1

INTRODUCTION TO BIOMETRICS

This chapter emphasize the significance of palmprint biometrics, Finger knuckle-print biometrics and their performance measures. Also the characteristics of local and global features are presented in this chapter.

1.1   Introduction

Biometrics refers to technologies for measuring and analyzing a person's physiological or behavioural characteristics (Wayman 2001). These characteristics are unique to individuals and it can be used to verify or identify a person. The applications of biometrics are considerably increased in the last years and it is expected in the near future. Depending on the deployment of biometrics, the applications are categorized in the following five main groups: forensic, government, commercial, health-care and travelling-immigration. However, some applications are common to these groups such as physical access, personal computer/network access, time and attendance, etc.

Biometrics has increasing attention in the e-world. Different types of biometrics were used in different applications. There are very few best biometric systems available in the market. The three different types of authentication are used in security system. The first type of authentication is password system and Postal Index Number (PIN) system. The second type of authentication is a card key, smart card or token system. The third type of authentication is a biometric technology. Out of these types of authentications in security system, biometric is the best secure and expedient authentication tool.

Biometrics cannot be easily borrowed, stolen or forgotten compared to the traditional security systems. The forgery of the biometric system is practically impossible. It refers to the person's unique physical or behavioural characteristics to distinguish or authenticate their own identity. The various physical biometrics are fingerprints (Belguechi et al 2013) hand or palm geometry (Matos et al 2012), retina (Hussain et al 2013), iris technique considers as a resemblance measure in certain biometrics systems (Miyazawa et al 2008), face (Yuchun et al 2002), palmprint (Sun et al 2005) hand vein (Huang et al 2013), palm vein (Venkat Narayana & Preethi 2010), finger knuckle-print (Nanni & Lumini 2009) or ear (Middendorff 2011). The behavioural biometrics is signature (Bertolini et al 2010), voice (Hollein 2002), keystroke pattern (Pin et al 2013) and gait (Hoang et al 2013).

1.1.1   Biometric Systems

The biometric trait can be acquired from an individual and then the feature set is extracted from the acquired data. Finally, this feature set is compared with the template set in the database. Therefore biometric system is also referred as a pattern recognition system. Biometric system may operate either in verification mode or identification mode based on the application it is used in the security system. In the verification mode, an individual's identity is authenticated in the security system by comparing the captured biometric trait with the own biometric template(s) stored in the system database. An individual may recognize one's identity with the help of PIN, a user name, or a smart card. Here the biometric system performs a one to one matching to determine whether person's individuality is correct or not. Identity verification is mainly used for positive recognition. The objective of the individuality verification is to avert several persons from consuming the similar uniqueness. The system recognizes an individual by searching in the verification templates of all the users in the database for a match in the identification approach. Therefore, the system performs a one-to-many matching to establish an individual's identity (or fails if the subject is not enrolled in the system database) without the subject having to claim an identity.

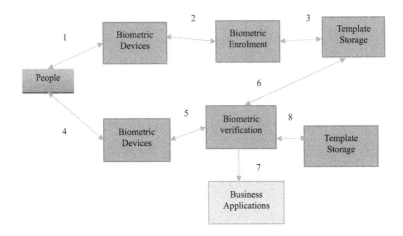

Figure 1.1 Working principle of biometric system (Simon & Mark 2001)

The various steps involved in Figure 1.1 (Simon & Mark 2001) are given below:

Step 1: Capture the chosen biometric;

Step 2: Process the biometric and extract and enroll the biometric templates;

Step 3: Store the template in a local repository, or a portable token such as a smart code;

Step 4: Live scan the chosen biometric;

Step 5: Process the biometric and extract the biometric template;

Step 6: Match the scanned biometric template against stored templates;

Step 7: Provide a matching score to business application;

Step 8: Record a secure audit trail with respect to system use.

The biometric system is divided into four main modules.

1. Sensor Module: It captures the biometric trait of a person.

2. Feature Extraction Module: The biometric trait obtained from the sensor module is processed to extract a set of or salient or discriminatory features.

3. Pattern Matching Module: The information mined in the feature extraction module is matched with the templates to generate the matching scores.

4. System database module: It is used in the biometric system to store the biometric templates of the enrolled users. The enrolment module is responsible for enrolling individuals in the biometric system database. The biometric reader is used to scan the biometric traits of an individual to produce the digital representation or feature values of the biometric characteristics during the enrolment phase. The data captured during the enrolment process may or may not be supervised by human depending on the application. An eminence testing is usually achieved to ensure that the acquired sample is relatively processed by successive stages. The feature extractor is used to process the digital representation for facilitate the matching to generate compact but expensive representation is called as template. The template is stored in the central database of a biometric system depending on the application. The templates are also recorded on a smart card issued to the individual. Usually, different templates of an individual are stored to account for variations observed in the biometric trait and the templates in the database may be updated over time.

The two different techniques to measure the biometric accuracy are the False Acceptance Rate (FAR) and False Rejection Rate (FRR). The limited entry is allowed to authorize the users by two methods focussed on the system's ability. The sensitivity of the mechanism is adjusted whatever matches to the biometrics. Based on that sensitivity, the biometric measures can vary significantly.

1.2   Palmprint Biometrics

Palmprint verification is implemented in different way compared to the fingerprint technology. The optical readers used in fingerprint technology are used in palmprint scanning. The size of the palmprint scanner is bigger. It has a limiting factor when used in workstations or mobile devices. The palms of the human hands contain pattern of ridges and valleys much like the fingerprints. The region of the palm is greatly higher than the region of a finger. Therefore palmprints are more distinctive than the fingerprints. The palmprint scanner is used to capture the large area of the palm. The low resolution scanner is used to capture the additional distinctive features such as principal lines and wrinkles in the palmprint. It is very cheap. Finally, it is used to capture all the features of the palmprint such as hand geometry, ridge and valley features (e.g., minutiae and singular points such as deltas), principal lines, and wrinkles.

Palmprint recognition inherently implements many of the same matching characteristics that have allowed fingerprint recognition to be one of the most well-known and best publicized biometrics. Both palm and finger biometrics is represented by the information presented in a friction ridge imprint. The palms and fingerprints are used as a trusted form of identification for more than a century. The image captured from the palm region of the hand refers to the palmprint. The image captured from a scanner or Charge Coupled Device (CCD) is known as online image. The image taken with the help of ink and paper are known as offline image. The palm itself consists of principal lines, wrinkles (secondary lines) and epidermal ridges. The palmprint features are different from fingerprint features.   The palmprint also contains other features such as indents and marks. These features are used to compare one palm with another palm. Palmprints are used for illegal, pathological, or profitable applications.

The palmprint pattern cannot duplicate with the other people, even in monozygotic twins. Hence palmprint is used as high reliable human identifier. The details of the palmprint ridges are stable. The information remains unchanged from

9

that time on throughout life, excluding for scope. After the demise, disintegration of the skin occurred lastly in the area of the palmprint. Matched with the other physical biometric features, palmprint verification has several benefits:

- Low-resolution imaging
- Low-intrusiveness
- Stable line features
- Low-cost capturing device

Palmprint covers wider area than fingerprint. It contains useful information for recognition. The dominant lines on the palmprint are known as three principal lines. The weaker and more irregular lines on the palm are known as wrinkles. The palmprint biometric system do not require very high resolution acquisition device. The principle lines and wrinkles are also acquired using low resolution acquisition device like 100 dpi (dots per inch) or lesser.

1.2.1   Preprocessing and ROI Extraction for Palmprint Biometrics

A palmprint region is extracted by pre-processing the acquired hand image. The square area inside the palm region of the hand image is considered as the palmprint or Region of Interest (ROI). Due to the regular and controlled uniform illumination conditions during image acquire, the attained hand image and its background contrast in colour. The sample input image is shown in the Figure 1.2(a), 1.3(a) and 1.4(a) for PolyU Palmprint database (Zhang et al 2003), COEP Palmprint database (Badrinath & Gupta 2010) and IIT - Delhi Palmprint database (Badrinath & Gupta 2010). The hand from the background is extracted by applying the Global Thresolding. Opening and Closing morphological operations is used to eliminate any isolated small blobs or holes. The contour of the hand image from the palmprint is acquired by applying the Contour-tracing algorithm. The ROI extraction for PolyU Palmprint database, COEP Palmprint database and IIT Delhi Palmprint database are the same as in (Rohit Khokher et al 2014) and of Figure 1.2(b) (Zhang et al 2003), 1.3(b) (Rohit Khokher et al 2014) and 1.4(b) (Badrinath & Gupta 2010) are shown respectively.

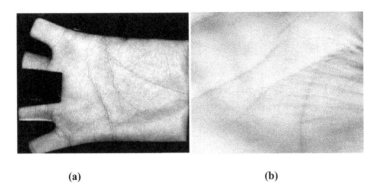

(a)   (b)

Figure 1.2 (a) Sample input image (Zhang et al 2003), (b) ROI image for PolyU palmprint database (Zhang et al 2003)

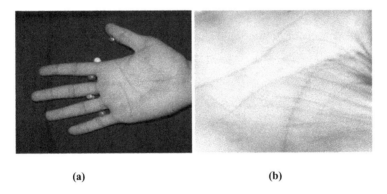

(a)   (b)

Figure 1.3 (a) Sample input image (Rohit Khokher et al 2014), (b) ROI image for COEP palmprint database (Rohit Khokher et al 2014)

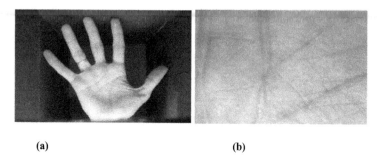

(a)   (b)

Figure 1.4 (a) Sample input image (Badrinath & Gupta 2010), (b) ROI image for IIT Delhi palmprint database (Badrinath & Gupta 2010)

1.3   Finger knuckle-print biometrics

The biometric analysts have less specialize in the Finger Knuckle-print (FKP) which is shown in the research field. The FKP biometric system provides a high level of security to human identifier. The image pattern of the skin on the rear surface of the finger is known as FKP. It is not a popular biometric recognition system compared to fingerprint biometrics system. The matching of finger knuckle patterns helps to spot the suspects and find out validating scientific proof from the images. Once if there is no information about fingerprints or face, then it is better among the market images. Choosing the biometrics is a challenging task for researcher. As it is contactless, there is chance for less proof of physical presence i.e. antispoofing. Finger knuckle-print has high textured region. Many samples are available per hand and independent to any behavioural aspect.

1.3.1   Finger Knuckle-print Anatomy

Each finger has three joints. The proximal phalanges, the centre phalanges and the distal phalanges are the three bones in each finger. The proximal phalanx is the first join where the finger gets join the hand. The Proximal Interphalangeal Joint

(PIP) is the second joint. The Distal Interphalangeal Joint (DIP) is the last joint of the finger as shown in Figure 1.5 (Kulkarni & Rout 2012). The image pattern of the skin on the back surface of the finger is known as the finger knuckle-print. The Finger knuckle is also known as dorsum of the hand. The inherent skin pattern of the outer surface around the phalange joint of one's finger has high capability to discriminate completely different people. Such image pattern of finger knuckle-print is unique and might be getting on-line, offline for authentication. Extraction of knuckle features for the identification is completely depends upon the user.

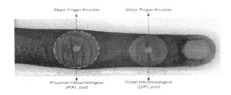

Figure 1.5 Finger knuckle-print anatomy (Sivaranjani et al 2014)

Several investigators of science mined the options for authentication as shown in Figure 1.6 (Kulkarni & Rout 2012). A pair of features in FKP is centre of phalange joint, U formed line round the middle phalanx, number of lines, length and spacing between lines. Knuckle crease patterns and stray marks are considered as a method of photographic identification. Such features are unique and it is used for an identification process.

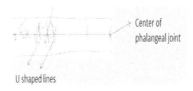

Figure 1.6 Finger knuckle print features (Kulkarni & Rout 2012)

The contact free imaging of the finger back surface is highly convenient to users. The images can also be acquired in online using either scanner or CCD camera. The acquired images are used to extract scale, translation and rotational invariant knuckle features for user identification (Kumar & Zhou 2009). It is reported that the skin pattern on the FKP is highly rich in texture due to skin wrinkles and creases and henceforth, it is measured as a biometric identifier. Further, advantages of using FKP include rich in texture information, simply available, contact-less image acquisition, invariant to emotions and other behavioural aspects such as fatigue, stable information and adequacy in the society. Despite of these characteristics and advantages of using FKP as biometric identifier, limited work are reported in the literature. The usage of finger knuckle for personal identification is shown in the ensuring results and generated a keen interest in biometrics. However, the research efforts to investigate the utility of finger knuckle patterns for personal identification were much restricted. As a result; there is no recognized use of knuckle pattern in commercial or civilian applications. The user acceptance for employing finger knuckle in human identification is expected to be very high (Kumar & Zhou 2009).

1.3.2   Preprocessing and ROI Extraction for Finger Knuckle-Print Biometrics

FKP images collected from different fingers are extremely assorted. The spatial locality is different for various FKP images. Therefore each FKP image is aligned by constructing the local coordinate system. Figure 1.7 (a) shows the FKP image sensor device (Zhang et al 2011) and Figure 1.7 (b) shows a sample finger knuckle-print image (Zhang et al 2011). Figure 1.8 (c) (Zhang et al 2011) and Figure 1.8 (d) shows ROI extraction technique and extracted image respectively (Zhang et al 2011).

14

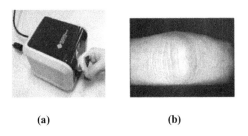

(a)   (b)

Figure 1.7 FKP (a) Image sensor device (Zhang et al 2011), (b) Sample image (Zhang et al 2011)

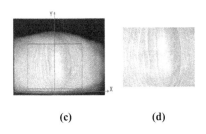

(c)   (d)

Figure 1.8 (c) ROI extraction technique (Zhang et al 2011), (d) ROI image (Zhang et al 2011)

1.4   Pros of finger knuckle-print and palmprint

- No expression, pose and ageing.
- No occlusion, less cooperation, inexpensive sensors.
- Cultivators and workers have equally good quality prints as others.
- No stigma of criminal investigation associated with palmprint and finger knuckle surface.
- Not easy to abrade.
- High user acceptance.

1.5   Local and Global features

Features extracted from the palmprint image are classified into local and global features. Local features characterize the main topological characteristics of a small part of the trajectory. Global features characterize the relationship of different line segments within a trajectory. The overall content and shape of the objects in the image represent the global features. The specific information in the local regions is defined as local features. The advantages of local features are defined in terms of template size and its discriminability. But the local features also have inevitable drawbacks in practical usage. Due to the sensitivity of the palmprint image, it is difficult to obtain the local features exactly. The performance of the local features gets degraded due to its poor palmprint quality and capture area. The global features represent the palmprint in a global perspective. Most of the global features are continuous and smooth everywhere expect in some special regions. The global features are extracted more consistently from the poor quality of the partial palmprints. It is too space and time consuming to directly store and compare the features pixel by pixel.

Global feature based matching overlaps two given templates with different transformation parameters and estimate the similarity score between the corresponding cells. Compared to local features, the global features have less distinctness and hence been often exploited together with the other features or in the pre-processing stage of palmprint matching. Both the local and global features are fairly independent. Further it captures the current information and hence it is realistic to improve the discriminating ability of matching by fusing features. The local and global features are combined in the matching stage with accessible feature level fusion strategies. The combined local and global features improve the performance of the palmprint systems on large scale databases. The selection of features is essential for the effective feature combination. The combination of irrelative features improves the accuracy or efficiency of the palmprint biometric systems. The suitable hierarchical approach is employed to reduce the additional time or memory cost required while fusing the local and global features.

1.6 Problem statement

The correct identity of the owners utilizing features computed from the data is established in the biometric system. Today subspace analysis methods are effective for face recognition but they may not be able to extract the distinctive line and junction features from the palmprint and FKP surface effectively. Therefore transform based methods are utilized for extracting both the local and global features from the palmprint and finger knuckle surface in evaluating the performance of the biometric system. The fusion of both local and global features provides higher recognition accuracy. Nowadays multi-scale, multi-resolution based techniques are being explored as potential candidates for efficient implementation of palmprint and FKP recognition.

1.7 Motivation

Palmprint and FKP based biometric approaches are intensively developed over the last few years because they possess several advantages over the other systems. Palmprint images are acquired with low resolution cameras and scanners and still consist of enough information to achieve good recognition rates. FKP has high textured region. Many samples are available for different hands and independent to any behavioural aspect. Palmprints and FKPs possess all the following properties such as universality, uniqueness, permanence, measurability, performance, acceptability, and circumvention. Overall, palmprint and finger knuckle-print based systems are well balanced in terms of cost and performance.

1.8   Objectives

Biometric methods for authenticating and identifying people are increasingly used in both the commercial and private sector. Today's commercially available biometric systems show good reliability. However, they generally lack user acceptance. Users showed an antipathy towards touching a possibly dirty fingerprint scanner, or looking into an iris scanner that might malfunction and eventually impair their vision. Whether those fears are well founded or not is less important. The fact is, they have considerable influence on user acceptance. And user consent is important for a good and successful application of a biometric system, as well as for good recognition rates. In response to the increasing demand for reliable as well as user friendly biometric systems, this work investigates the applicability of palmprint and FKP were the biometric features for authentication. Using palmprint or FKP as a biometric system avoid such problems as shown before, since it requires no subject interaction.

The main objectives of the thesis are

- To propose the transform based techniques that is used to achieve higher recognition accuracy and lower equal error rate

- To examine the performance of the proposed techniques with the existing methodologies

1.9   Biometric Datasets
1.9.1   College of Engineering – Pune (COEP) Palmprint Datasets

The COEP palmprint database (COEP Palm Print Database (College of Engineering Pune) 2010) consists of 8 different images of single person's palm. The database consists of total 1344 images pertaining to 168 persons. The dataset is collected over a period of one year. The images were captured using digital camera. The resolution of images is 1600×1200 pixels.

1.9.2   The PolyU Palmprint Datasets

The PolyU Palmprint Database (Zhang 2010) contains 7752 gray scale images corresponding to 386 different palms in BMP (Bitmap) image format. Twenty samples are collected from each of these palms in two sessions. Each 10 samples were captured in the first session and the session, correspondingly. The average intermission among the first and the second collection is two months period of time.

1.9.3   Indian Institute of Technology (IIT Delhi) Touchless Palmprint Datasets

The IIT-Delhi palmprint image database (Kumar 2007) consists of the hand images collected from the students and staff at IIT-Delhi, India. This dataset is acquired in the IIT Delhi campus during July 2006 - Jun 2007 using a simple and touchless imaging setup. The images are collected in the indoor atmosphere and employ circular fluorescent illumination around the camera lens. The presently accessible dataset is from 235 users. All the subjects in the database are in the age group 12-57 years. In each subject, seven images are collected from each of the left and right hand. All the images were collected in fluctuating hand posture differences. All the subjects are offered with live feedback to present the person's hand in the imaging region. The touchless imaging consequences in higher image scale variations. The resolution of these images is 800 × 600 pixels and all these images are available in bitmap format. Finally 150 × 150 pixels are automatically cropped and normalized palmprint images are also available.

1.9.4   The PolyU Finger Knuckle-Print Datasets

PolyU FKP database (Zhang 2009) consists of 7920 images collected from 660 different fingers. The samples are collected in two separate sessions. In each session; six images are collected for the left index and left middle finger, the right

19

index and right middle finger. From each person, 48 images are collected from 4 fingers. The size of the acquired FKP images is 768×576 under resolution above 400 dpi. Based on the experiments, high resolution images are not necessary for feature extraction and pattern matching. Therefore, Gaussian smoothing operation is applied to the original image. The smoothen image is down sampled to about 150 dpi. Hence the size of ROI images is 110×220 pixels.

1.10 Performance Metrics

Performance testing comprises a critical aspect of biometric modality assessments. Investigators are able to draw from a wide range of performance evaluation metrics that assess functional system accuracy and usability. The choice of metrics employed in performance testing is considered by the type of biometric modality or system undergoing evaluation precisely, whether the scheme is traditional in nature (i.e. a well-established, single transaction identification modality such as Fingerprint, Face, or Iris recognition) or novel in nature (e.g. an emerging modality such as Pulse, or an innovative application such as cognitive biometrics).

Traditional performance metrics describe system accuracy, precision and usability. The ability of an authentication system to measure a biometric with a high degree of closeness to the biometrics' true value is known as accuracy. The repeatability of accurate system measurements over time is known as precision. The ease with which a system used is termed as usability. The majority of traditional biometric performance metrics derives from signal detection theory. It seeks to quantify the ability to discern between information-bearing energy patterns (signals) and the random energy patterns (noise) that obstruct the informative pattern detection and acquisition. Traditional biometric performance metrics are referred and applied in a variety of ways, taking into consideration: performance evaluation type (technical, scenario, or operational testing), performance component assessment (detection, acquisition, enrollment, matching, and authentication), human factors (usability), and others.

The performance of a biometric feature, result or application is distinguished by dissimilar metrics. The user needs to enroll his biometric traits when the biometric system is used for the first time. The biometric scheme needs palmprints, finger knuckle-print from the operator. This input is stored in the database as a template. It is internally linked to a User ID (Identification). The biometric input is matched with the templates in the database by a pattern matching algorithm when the user wants to authenticate or identify the person for the first time.

Performance metrics generally take the system of rates for each metric. It is important to note that the measured/observed rate in any evaluation is distinct from the predicted/expected rate that occurs in deployed, fully operational biometric systems (predicted/expected performance rates may be gauged using measured/observed rates).

1.10.1 False Acceptance Rate and False Rejection Rate

The probability that the system incorrectly authorizes an unauthorized individual due to wrongly matching the biometric input with a template is known as False Acceptance Rate. The FAR is normally expressed as a percentage of invalid inputs which are incorrectly accepted. False Accept Rate is also called as False Match Rate.

The false acceptance rate describes the proportion of identification or verification transactions in which an impostor subject is incorrectly matched to a genuine user template stored within a biometric system. FAR reflects the ability of a non-authorized user to access a system, whether via zero-effort access attempts or deliberate spoofing or the other methods of circumvention.

The probability that the system incorrectly rejects the access to an authorized individual due to deteriorating the wrong match is known as the false rejection rate. The FRR is normally expressed as a percentage of valid inputs which are incorrectly rejected. FAR and FRR are much dependent in the biometric factor and the technical implementation of the biometric solution. A personal FRR is determined for each individual because FRR is purely person dependent. Take this into account while determining the FRR of a biometric solution; one person is insufficient to establish an overall FRR for a solution. Due to environmental conditions or incorrect use, for example when using dirty palmprints on a palmprint reader, the FRR is increased. Mostly the FRR lowers when a user gains more experience in using the biometric device or software. False Reject Rate is sometimes referred as False Non-Match Rate.

The FRR describes the proportion of identification or verification transactions in which a genuine subject is incorrectly rejected from a biometric system. FRR may occur as a result of user presentation error or the exploitation of formerly enrolled authentication templates.

FAR and FRR are the key metrics for biometric solutions, certain biometric devices or software even allow to tune them so that the system more quickly matches or rejects. Both FRR and FAR are significant, but for greatest applications one of them is considered as most important. Two examples to exemplify this:

1. When biometrics is used for logical or physical admittance control, the objective of the application is to prohibit access to unauthorized individuals in all situations. It is strong that a very low FAR is desirable for such an application, even if it comes at the cost of a higher FRR.

2. When surveillance cameras are used to screen a crowd of people for missing children, the objective of the application is to identify any missing offspring that come up on the screen. When the identification of those offspring is computerised using a face recognition software, this software has to be set up with a low FRR. As such a greater quantity of matches will be false positives, but these are studied rapidly by surveillance personnel.

22

1.10.2 Speed

The time taken to enroll the people in the template and the time taken by an individual to be authenticated is given by the manufacturers of biometric devices and software.

1.10.3 Equal Error Rate (EER)

The equal error rate describes the point at which genuine and imposter error rates are closest to zero. EER can be represented as a percentage with time/unit factors (e.g. results of "8.3% EER for 1sec/1heartbeat" in a Pulse modality study). EER is not beneficial in considering definite scheme performance, but can be helpful as a first-order performance indicator for 1:1 verification systems.

1.10.4 Correct Classification Rate (CCR)

Classification accuracy depicts, very commonly, the proportion of profiles that is correctly matched to users. The correct classification rate metric often appears in studies involving very small data sets - e.g. 100% classification accuracy achieved in one among the five person EEG study.

1.10.5 Data Presentation Curves

In addition to rate-based metrics, different types of data presentation curves are commonly used to describe and model biometric performance. Matching and authentication performance metrics are used to understand system capabilities and determine what types of systems are best meet to the requirements of a given use case. The different types of data presentation curves are used to describe and model the matching and authentication performance of novel biometric systems.

1.10.5.1   Receiver Operating Characteristic (ROC) Curve

A ROC curve plots of the rate of false positives (accepted impostor attempts) along the x-axis against the corresponding rate of true positives (genuine attempts accepted) on the y-axis; points are plotted parametrically as a function of the decision threshold. A ROC curve plots FAR (accepted impostor attempts) along the x-axis against the corresponding rate of true positives (genuine attempts accepted) on the y-axis; points are plotted parametrically as a function of the decision threshold.

CHAPTER 2

FINGER KNUCKLE-PRINT IDENTIFICATION BASED ON LOCAL AND GLOBAL FEATURE EXTRACTION USING FAST DISCRETE ORTHONORMAL STOCKWELL TRANSFORM

This chapter highlight the overview of Fast Discrete Orthonormal Stockwell Transform is explained. A brief review of local and global extraction techniques and Phase only correlation, Band Limited phase only correlation techniques are also presented.

2.1 Overview of Fast Discrete orthonormal Stockwell transform

The DOST is calculated in a faster manner by taking advantage of the FFT. The Fast Discrete Orthonormal Stockwell Transform of a signal $h(t)$) is defined as:

$$S_{[v,\beta,\tau]} = \frac{1}{\sqrt{\beta}} \sum_{f=v-\beta/2}^{v+\beta/2-1} exp(-i\pi\tau)exp\left(i2\pi\frac{\tau}{\beta}f\right)H[f] \tag{2.1}$$

where the value of f is summed only on a certain band (depending on v and β). Hence, this summation is represented by the inner product between a row in a sparse matrix and the vector of the Fourier coefficients, H.

2.2 Local – Global Feature Extraction and Matching

2.2.1 Local Feature

The feature extraction technique of finger knuckle-print biometric system is used to obtain good inter-class separation in least time. The features of finger knuckle-print are extracted by using Fast Discrete Orthonormal Stockwell transform after the completion of pre-processing and ROI segmentation from finger knuckle-print. The ROI image is shown in Figure 2.1 (Zhang et al 2011). The local variation of instantaneous-phase is used to extract features from finger knuckle-print. Instantaneous phase obtained using FDOST is resolution of phase with respect to

25

time. It is more informative of signal compared to only phase or amplitude representation. Therefore, the instantaneous-phase features are more discriminant compared to only amplitude or phase features. Therefore, instantaneous-phase is utilized for extracting finger knuckle-print features in the proposed system identifies the user with more probability in bulk database of users. The extracted features from the live finger knuckle-print are matched with features of registered finger knuckle-print features stored in the database for verification and identification. This technique uses the nearest-neighbour approach to match the live and enrolled finger knuckle-print. If both live and matched finger-knuckle print are from same class, then it is considered to be a genuine (Non-False) match, otherwise it is treated as an imposter (False) match. The distance between the features is calculated using Hamming distance.

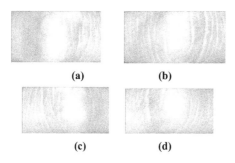

(a)   (b)

(c)   (d)

Figure 2.2 FKP ROI images for PolyU database from (a) Left index fingers (Zhang et al 2011 (b) Left middle fingers (Zhang et al 2011 (c) Right index fingers (Zhang et al 2011and (d) Right middle fingers (Zhang et al 2011

2.2.2 Global Feature

Fast Discrete Orthonormal Stockwell transform is used to extract the instantaneous phase information and also it is considered as a windowed Fourier transform. Band-Limited Phase Only Correlation is used to match the global feature of two FKP images. A matching is accomplished between a pair of finger knuckle-

26

print images from the same hand for genuine matching and hence BLPOC shows a much sharper peak than Phase Only Correlation. Figure 2.2, 2.3, 2.4 and 2.5 shows an example of image matching using POC function. A matching is performed between couples of finger knuckle-print images from different hand for imposter matching. Both the BLPOC and POC never exhibit a divergent cruel peak. The displacement between finger knuckle-print ROI images is aligned using BLPOC. The closeness between Fourier transforms of the aligned RoIs is measured using BLPOC. A genuine matching and an imposter matching using BLPOC function is shown in Figure 2.6 (Author's own work), 2.7 (Author's own work), 2.8 (Author's own work) and 2.9 (Author's own work).

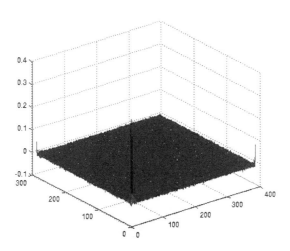

Figure 2.3 POC function of FKP ROI images for PolyU database from left index fingers using FDOST (Author's own work)

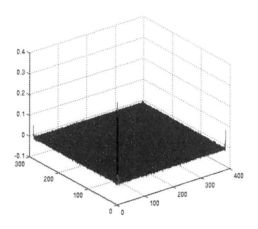

Figure 2.4 POC function of FKP ROI images for PolyU database from left middle fingers using FDOST (Author's own work)

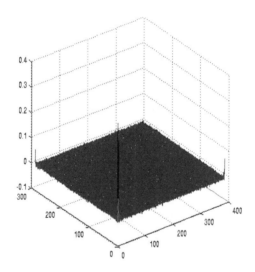

Figure 2.5 POC function of FKP ROI images for PolyU database from right index fingers using FDOST (Author's own work)

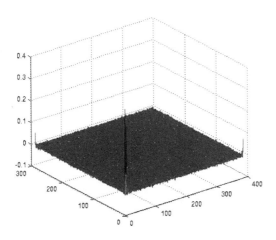

Figure 2.6 POC function of FKP ROI images for PolyU database from right middle fingers using FDOST (Author's own work)

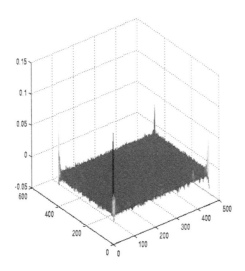

Figure 2.7 BLPOC function of FKP ROI images for PolyU database from left index fingers using FDOST (Author's own work)

29

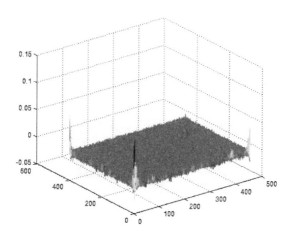

Figure2.8   BLPOC function of FKP ROI images for PolyU database from left
middle fingers using FDOST (Author's own work)

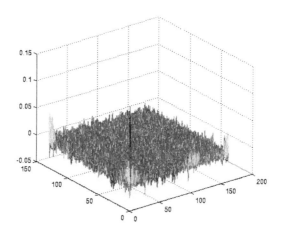

Figure 2.9   BLPPOC function of FKP ROI images for PolyU database from
right index fingers using FDOST (Author's own work)

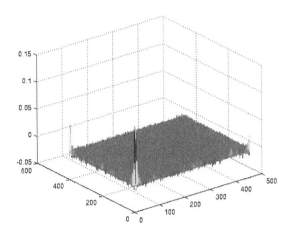

Figure 2.10 BLPOC function of FKP ROI images for PolyU database from right middle fingers using FDOST (Author's own work)

2.3 Local global information fusion for knuckle-print recognition

The ratio between the general region area and the area of the original ROI is checked in the finger knuckle-print system. Then two finger knuckle-print ROI images are matched and the matching distance is calculated. The peak value of BLPOC function between finger knuckle-print ROI images is used to measure the similarity of their Fourier transform. Finally the two matching distances were obtained by combining the two distances using two different matchers. Maximum weighted rule is used to assign the weights for fusing the two matching distances obtained. Finally the fused final matching distance is estimated.

2.4 Experimental results and discussion

Performance of the proposed technique is measured using the selected FKP ROI images extracted from the hand images of the separate databases. The

31

uniqueness of the individual is compared with the biometric trait in the biometric verification system. If the uniqueness of the individual claimed and the biometric trait matching is closer, then the match score is higher the matching score. An individual authentication is accepted if the match score exceeds a given threshold. The accuracy is calculated through three parameters such as False Rejection Rate, False Acceptance Rate and Genuine Acceptance Rate. The percentage of a query that is identified as no match is termed as False Rejection Rate. The fraction of queries that are identified mistakenly as other objects is called as False Acceptance Rate. The fraction of the queries that are correctly recognized is defined as Genuine Acceptance Rate. Due to the difficulties of collecting samples of finger knuckle-print images and long running time of the large finger knuckle-print dataset in the schemes, the proposed scheme is tested on a lesser amount of samples. A test is conducted by changing the size of the gallery samples of each person from 1 to 15. From 1 to 15 images per finger knuckle-print are taken for training data. ROC is a plot of Genuine Acceptance Rate against False Acceptance Rate shown in Figure 2.10 (Author's own work), 2.11 (Author's own work), 2.12 (Author's own work) and 2.13 (Author's own work). Hence, the investigational results show that the fusing local and global information together performs better than the methods in the previous works depending on the local and global features independently.

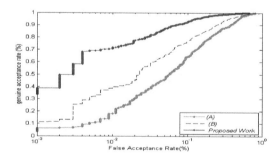

Figure 2.11 ROC Curves of FKP images for PolyU database from left index fingers using FDOST (Author's own work)

32

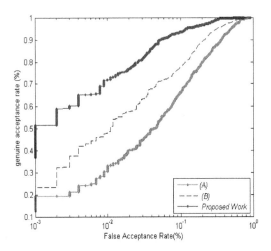

Figure 2.12 ROC Curves of FKP images for PolyU database from left middle fingers using FDOST (Author's own work)

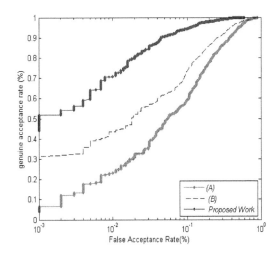

Figure 2.13 ROC Curves of FKP images for PolyU database from right index fingers using FDOST (Author's own work)

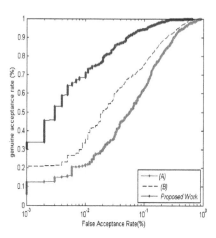

Figure 2.14 ROC Curves of FKP images for PolyU database from right middle fingers using FDOST (Author's own work)

The Distance distributions of genuine matching's and imposter matching's acquired by proposed scheme are plotted as shown in Figure 2.14 (Author's own work), 2.15 (Author's own work), 2.16 (Author's own work) and 2.17(Author's own work).

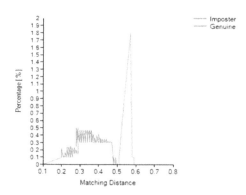

Figure 2.15 Distance distributions of genuine matching's and imposter matching's of FKP for PolyU database from left index fingers using FDOST (Author's own work)

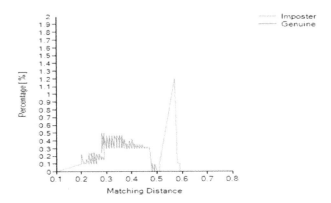

Figure 2.16 Distance distributions of genuine matching's and imposter matching's of FKP for PolyU database from left middle fingers using FDOST(Author's own work)

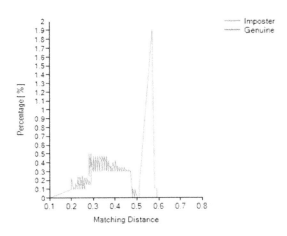

Figure 2.17 Distance distributions of genuine matching's and imposter matching's of FKP for PolyU database from right index fingers using FDOST (Author's own work)

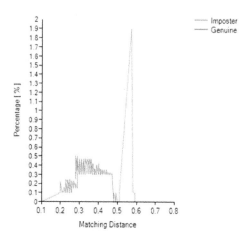

Figure 2.18 Distance distributions of genuine matching's and imposter matching's of FKP for PolyU database from right index fingers using FDOST (**Author's own work**)

EERS (%) By different schemes is shown in Table 5.1. It is observed from Table 5.1 that the propsoed system has low EER comapred to the existing systems. Hence the proposed system outperforms than the existing systems. Table 5.2 shows the performance measures of the proposed system.

Table 2.1 EERS (%) By different schemes and FDOST

Finger Type	CompCode (A)	LGIC (B)	Proposed work
Left index	2.06	1.65	1.15
Left middle	1.96	1.45	1.06
Right index	1.82	1.37	1.14
Right middle	1.87	1.39	1.05

Table 2.2 Performance measures of the proposed FDOST

Finger Type	CRR (%)	EER (%)	DI
Left index	99.20	1.15	5.86
Left middle	99.35	1.06	5.74
Right index	99.46	1.14	5.82
Right middle	99.24	1.05	5.71

2.5 Summary

The acquired FKP images are preprocessed and ROI is extracted. The Fast Discrete Orthonormal Stockwell transform is used to extract the local features. This transform method is used as the local feature extractor method. The Fast Discrete Orthonormal Stockwell transform is increased to infinity to obtain the Fourier transform of the image. The local features are matched using minimum distance classifier. Then the Fourier transform coefficients are utilized as the global feature. The global features are matched by using Band Limited Phase only correlation. Finally, both the features are combined to obtain high recognition accuracy. The experimental results show that the proposed work performs better than the existing works.

CHAPTER 3

CONCLUSIONS AND FUTURE WORK

3.1   SUMMARY AND CONCLUSIONS

Palmprint recognition is a biometric technology which recognizes a person based on a person's palmprint pattern. The palmprint patterns are not duplicated with other people, even in monozygotic twins. Hence palmprint is used as high reliable human identifier. The user acceptance for employing finger knuckle in human identification is expected to be very high as there is no stigma of personal information (such as life-line, heart-line, head-line associated with palm surface) associated with finger knuckle lines/creases. The principal lines in the palmprint do not adequately to provide high recognition accuracy because of their similarity among different palms. Accurately extracting wrinkles in the palmprint is still difficult task. Subspace analysis methods may be effective for face recognition but they may not be able to effectively extract the distinctive line and junction features from the palmprint and finger knuckle surface. To address this problem, a research issue named transform based techniques is proposed. In this thesis, the current research literature on the various methods for feature extraction and pattern matching algorithms is reviewed and analyzed extensively.

POC and BLPOC based method is developed to match the two finger knuckle-print to improve the accuracy of the developed biometric system. The instantaneous phase features were extracted by three feature extraction methods for the publicly available finger knuckle-print databases.

The features extracted by using these methods like FDOST were called as local features. Hence these methods are called as the local feature extractor. The Fourier coefficients that are extracted by these methods are known as the global features. These methods were also called as Global feature extractor methods. The local features are matched by using distance classifier. The global features are matched by POC and BLPOC

38

matcher. The two distance obtained from these two matchers are fused based on the Maximum Weighted (MW) rule. The experimental results show significant improvements in the authentication performance when compared with existing systems.

Images of Finger Knuckle-print traits are obtained from publicly available biometric databases such as PolyU Finger Knuckle-print Database. The performance of the proposed biometric systems are evaluated using measures like Genuine Acceptance Rate (GAR), False Acceptance Rate (FAR), False Rejection Rate (FRR), Correct Recognition Rate(CRR), Equal Error Rate (EER) and Decidability Index(DI).

The CRR, EER and DI of FKP biometric systems using FDOST are 99.20%, 1.15%, and 5.86 (left index), 99.35%, 1.06%, 5.74 (left middle), 99.46%, 1.14%, 5.82 (right index) 99.24%, 1.05% and 5.71 (right middle) for PolyU Database.

The existing transform based techniques does not use Time Frequency Representation (TFR). But the proposed system uses the TFR analysis while extracting the features. Hence the proposed work performs better than the related works interms of EER.

3.2 FUTURE WORKS

Biometrics systems were widely used currently in almost all safety related automation applications. Hence the performance of the biometric systems needs to improve. Following are the few considerations of future works that are extended or implemented for the biometric authentication system.

- Fuzzy binary decision tree classifier, SVM classifier are utilized to improve the recognition accuracy of the biometric databases.

- Ant Colony Optimization and Particle Swarm Optimization algorithm were implemented to optimize the features fused at fusion strategy.

- Zak transform are utilized to extract the local and global features in biometric traits like palmprint, finger knuckle-print and hand vein in future.

REFERENCES

1. Aoyama, S, Ito, K & Aoki, T 2014, 'A finger-knuckle-print recognition algorithm using phase-based local block matching', Information Sciences, vol. 268, pp. 53–64.

2. Badrinath, GS & Gupta, P 2010, 'Stockwell transform based palm-print recognition', Applied Soft Computing, vol. 11, no. 7, pp. 4267-4281.

3. Belguechi, R, Cherrier, E, Rosenberger, C & Ait-Aoudia, S 2013, 'Operational bio-hash to preserve privacy of fingerprint minutiae templates', IET Biometrics, vol. 2, no. 2, pp. 76-84.

4. Bertolini, D, Oliveira, LS, Justino, E & Sabourin, R 2010, 'Reducing forgeries in writer-independent off-line signature verification through ensemble of classifier', Pattern Recognition, vol. 43, no. 1, pp. 387-396.

5. COEP Palm Print Database (College of Engineering Pune). 2010. Available from : <http://www.coep.org>

6. Drabycz, S, Stockwell, RG & Ross Mitchell, J 2009, 'Image Texture Characterization using the Discrete Orthonormal S-transform', Journal of Digital Imaging, vol. 22, no. 6, pp. 696-708.

7. Hoang, T, Nguyen, T, Luong, C, Do, S & Choi, D 2013, 'Adaptive Cross-Device Gait Recognition Using a Mobile Accelerometer', Journal of Information Processing Systems, vol. 9, no. 2, pp. 333-348.

8. Hollein, HF 2002, Forensic Voice Identification, Academic Press.

9. Huang, D, Tang, Y, Wang, Y, Chen, L & Wang, Y 2013, 'Hand vein recognition based on oriented gradient maps and local feature matching', Computer Vision, Lecture Notes in Computer Science, vol. 7727, no. 430-444, pp. 430-444.

10. Hussain, A, Bhuiyan, A, Mian, A & Ramamohanarao, K 2013, Biometric Security Application for Person Authentication Using Retinal Vessel Feature : proceeding of the International Conference on Digital Image Computing: Techniques and Application, pp. 1-8.

11. Ito, K, Aoki, T, Nakajima, H, Kobayashi, K & Higuchi, T 2008, 'A palmprint recognition algorithm using phase-only correlation', IEICE Transactions on Fundamentals of Electronics, Communications and Computer Sciences, vol. E91-A, no. 4, pp. 1023-1030.

12. Ito, K, Nakajima, H, Kobayashi, K, Aoki, T & Higuch, T 2004, 'A fingerprint matching algorithm using phase-only correlation', IEICE Transactions on

Fundamentals of Electronics, Communications and Computer Sciences, vol. E87-A, no. 3, pp. 682-691.

13. Kulkarni, SS & Rout, RD 2012, 'Secure Biometrics: Finger Knuckle Print', International Journal of Advanced Research in Computer and Communication Engineering, vol. 1, no. 10, pp. 852-854.

14. Kumar 2007, Palmprint Image Database version1, IIT, Delhi, India. Available from : <http://www4.comp.polyu.edu.hk/~csajaykr/IITD/DatabasePalm.htm> [July 2010].

15. Kumar, R, Ratnesh, P, Keshri, C, Malathy & Annapoorani Panaiyappan, K 2010, 'Motion invariant palm-print texture based biometric security', Procedia Computer Science, vol. 2, pp. 159-163.

16. Kumar, A & Zhou, Y 2009, Human identification using knuckle codes : proceeding of the 3rd IEEE international conference on Biometrics: Theory, applications and systems, pp. 147-152.

17. Kumar, A & Zhou, Y 2009, 'Personal identification using finger knuckle orientation features', Electronics Letters, vol. 45, no. 20, pp. 1023-1025.

18. Matos, H, Oliveira, HP & Magalhaes, F 2012, 'Hand-geometry based recognition system-A Non Restricted Acquisition Approach', Image Analysis and Recognition, Lecture Notes in Computer Science, vol. 7325, pp. 38-45.

19. McFadden, PD, Cook, JG & Forste, LM 1999, 'Decomposition of gear vibration signals by the generalized S-transform', Mechanical Systems and Signal Processing, vol. 13, no. 5, pp. 691-707.

20. Middendorff, C 2011, Multi-Biometric Approaches to Ear Biometrics and Soft Biometrics, BiblioBazaar.

21. Miyazawa, K, Ito, K, Aoki, T, Kobayashi, K & Nakajima, N 2008, 'An effective approach for Iris recognition using phase-based image matching', IEEE Transactions on Pattern Analysis and Machine Intelligence, vol. 30, no. 10, pp. 1741-1756.

22. Nanni, L & Lumini, A 2009, 'A multi-matcher system based on knuckle-based features', Neural Computing and Applications, vol. 18, no. 1, pp. 87-91.

23. Pin, ST, Jin Teoh, AB & Yue, S 2013, 'A Survey of Keystroke Dynamics Biometrics', The Scientific World Journal, vol. 2013, pp. 1-25.

24. Pinnegar, CR & Eaton, DW 2003, 'Application of the S transform to prestack noise attention filtering', Journal of Geophysical Research, vol. 108, no. B9, pp. 2422-2431.

25. Rohit K, Ram CS & Rahul K 2014, 'Palmprint Recoginition Using Geometrical and Texture Properties', 2nd International Conference on Research in Science, Engineering and Technology (ICRSET'2014), Dubai (UAE).

26. Sejdi, E, Djurovi, I & Jiang, J 2008, 'A Window Width Optimized S-Transform', EURASIP Journal on Advances in Signal Processing, pp. 1-19.

27. Simon, L, & Marki, S, 2001, 'A Practical Guide to Biometric Security Technology', IEEE Security, pp. 27-32.

28. Sivaranjani, B, & Yamini , C & Jackulin Durairani, A, 2014, 'A Literature Study on Finger Knuckle Matching Techniques', International Journal for Research in Emerging Science and Technology, vol. 1, no. 6, pp. 47-52.

29. Stankovic, LJ 2001, 'A Measure of some time-frequency distributions concentration', Signal Processing, vol. 81, no. 3, pp. 621-631.

30. Stockwell, RG, Mansinha, L & Lowe, RP 1996, 'Localization of the complex spectrum: the S transform', IEEE Transactions on Signal Processing, vol. 44, no. 4, pp. 998-1001.

31. Sun, Z, Tan, T, Wang, Y & Li, SZ 2005, Ordinal palmprint represention for personal identification : proceeding of the IEEE Computer Society Conference on Computer Vision and Pattern Recognition, pp. 279-284.

32. Su, Y, Shan, S, Chen, X & Gao, W 2009, 'Hierarchical ensemble of global and local classifiers for face recognition', IEEE Transactions on Image Processing, vol. 18, no. 8, pp. 1885-1896.

33. Usha, K & Ezhilarasan, M 2013, A Competent Method for Personal Authentication based on Intra-Knuckle Parameter : proceeding of the International Conference on Advances in Information Technology and Mobile Communication, pp. 269-276.

34. Venkat Narayana, T & Preethi, K 2010, 'Future of Human Security Based on Computational Intelligence Using Palm Vein Technology', International Journal of Computer Science and Emerging Technologies, vol. 1, no. 1, pp. 68-73.

35. Wayman, J 2001, 'Fundamentals of Biometric Authentication Technologies', International Journal of Image and Graphics, vol. 1, no. 1, pp. 93-113.

36. Xu, X, Guo, Z, Song, C & Li, Y 2012, 'Multispectral Palmprint Recognition Using a Quaternion Matrix', Sensors, vol. 12, pp. 4633-4647.

37. Yuchun, F, Tieniu, T & Wang, Y 2002, Fusion of global and local features for face verification : proceeding of the 16th International Conference on Pattern Recognition, pp. 382-385.

38. Zhang 2009, The Hong Kong Polytechnic University (PolyU), Finger-Knuckle-Print Database. Available from : <http://www4.comp.polyu.edu.hk/~biometrics/FKP.htm> [July 2010].

39. Zhang 2010, HongKong Polytechnic University, PolyU Palmprint Database. Available from : <http://www4.comp.polyu.edu.hk/~biometrics> [July 2010].

40. Zhang, D, Kong, WK, You, J & Wong, M 2003, 'Online palmprint identification', IEEE Transactions on Pattern Analysis and Machine Intelligence, vol. 25, no. 9, pp. 1041-1050.

41. Zhang, L, Zhang, L, Zhang, D & Zhu, H 2011, 'Ensemble of local and global information for finger–knuckle-print recognition', Pattern Recognition, vol. 44, no. 9, pp. 1990-1998.

42. Zhang, XD & Bao, Z 2001, The non-stationary signal analysis and processing, National Defense Industry Press, Beijing.